T0199121

A Workbook for
Estate Administrators

Til Death
Do We
Part

Kimberly Jenkins

WESTBOW
PRESS®
A DIVISION OF THOMAS NELSON
& ZONDERVAN

WestBow Press books may be ordered through booksellers or by contacting:

WestBow Press
A Division of Thomas Nelson & Zondervan
1663 Liberty Drive
Bloomington, IN 47403
www.westbowpress.com
1 (866) 928-1240

ISBN: 978-1-5127-6064-4 (sc)
ISBN: 978-1-5127-6065-1 (e)

Library of Congress Control Number: 2016917234

Print information available on the last page.

WestBow Press rev. date: 12/9/2016

CONTENTS

        Worksheets: Twenty-four months of calendars; Message pad sheets to keep track of conversations, dates, and times; Mileage reports; Time Sheet; Expense Report; Petty cash journal pages; Petty cash vouchers; To Do List with who owns the task and target date of completion. If you need more, just photocopy the worksheets as you go through the process, but whatever you do, make sure to keep them all in your binder so you don't lose or misplace anything. Worksheets may be downloaded from my author website, resources tab http://www.kimberlyjenkinsauthor.com.

I dedicate this workbook to my auntie, Dee Ward, who was so sweet and kind, so brave in the face of a horribly aggressive disease and the very difficult treatments it necessitated, yet had the grace and dignity to prepare and plan as best she could for my sister and me to tidy up things nicely and neatly upon her death. To my auntie—I pray you are in heaven with my momma, giggling and enjoying eternity, in a new body, in full wellness and relationship with the Lord. Thank you for the blessing of this experience, and please know we did our best in executing your wishes to the letter. The bishop did a wonderful job with your service, your sweet little dog is with a happy family, and thank you for the note you left us in your computer room. We found it right before we flew back home. May your hand be in the publishing and distribution of this workbook. A portion of each sale will, of course, go to charity, so we can keep the blessing flowing even after you're gone. Rest in peace, Auntie. Find me when I get there!

VI

If you were coming in the fall,
I'd brush the summer by
With half a smile and half a spurn,
As housewives do a fly

If I could see you in a year,
I'd wind the months in balls,
And put them each in separate drawers,
Until their time befalls.

If only centuries delayed,
I'd count them on my hand,
Subtracting 'til my fingers dropped
Into Van Diemen's land.

If certain, when this life was out,
That yours, and mine should be,
I'd toss it yonder like a rind,
And taste eternity.

But now, all ignorant of the length,
Of times uncertain wing,
It goads me, like a goblin bee,
That will not state its sting.

Emily Dickinson, "Love VI"
The Complete Poems of Emily Dickinson, 1924

PREFACE

The purpose of this book is twofold. Some will use it to record their personal information that will be needed after their death. Then another person, the estate administrator, will use this book as a workbook to finalize the original preparer's wishes after his or her death. For the estate administrator, the workbook will be used and referred to on a daily basis, in order to assist with closing down the affairs of the original preparer. You will keep this book with you and refer to it on just about every occasion; you will insert copies of receipts and documents you will have to prepare as you work through the process. You may want to purchase a three-ring binder, some tabs, and a three-hole punch so you can insert your completed worksheets shown here in the appendix section, or download them from my website at www.KimberlyJenkinsauthor.com. I would purchase some sleeves with envelopes to go into the book under the particular sections you will be working with. It's easier if you follow a logical path in the order we have laid out. In the appendix section at the end of this book, you will find a shopping list you can take with you to the office supply store. This will help you get all the supplies you will need as you set out on this journey.

To the preparer of this book I say, *this book is **not** a last will and testament, nor is it meant to be considered legal or accounting advice. It does not supersede any legal documents put in place by you, the preparer, but instead acts as a treasure map to find all the things one will need to process your estate.*

I make reference to two people in the book, the "preparer" (the person who is alive and entering their information into the book for future use by another) and the "administrator" (the person or persons who will use this book as a guide to tidy up the affairs of the preparer).

The preparer will three-hole punch and insert copies of various documents and perhaps some handwritten notes. The administrator will use the worksheet in the back to document everything, including telephone calls, expense reports, petty cash, and mileage.

I am convinced the time to complete this book is when you are well. If you wait until you are ill, you may not feel like completing the spreadsheets. If you wait until you are gravely ill, your mind may not be able to recall the details you will want to note, and the preparation of your final affairs may add to your anxiety of being gravely ill. If you complete, or at least start, the book when you are well, it is a much easier task to just update the existing material.

I know this book goes against the grain of conventional thinking. We have spent all our lives trying to secure our passwords, keep private our account information, and so forth, but in doing so, we may only be locking out our loved ones and making their job as administrators more difficult. So with that in mind, keep the workbook secure, but let your administrator know you have it and where to find it upon your death. Surely if someone offers to do this task for you, which will take a year or so of his or her life, the least you can do is make it as easy for him or her as possible. So secure the book once it is complete.

ACKNOWLEDGMENTS

It is with a truly grateful heart that I extend my deepest gratitude to the multiple people who assisted me in this venture. To Aunt Dee, who asked me to be the coexecutor of her estate and lead me down this path initially. To Bishop Peter Robinson of the St. Paul's Anglican church, who executed my aunt's service and was a pillar of strength while my sister and I were in Arizona trying to get through a funeral, estate sale, and home sale. To my sister, Laurie Widener, who walked this journey with me and prayed with me before, during, and after. To Maurice Broaddus, my WestBow publishing consultant, for getting me started. To Chris Varques, my WestBow check-in coordinator, for keeping me on task and motivated to meet my deadlines. Your gentle nudges with a happy voice kept me on task on days when I wasn't feeling so motivated. To my editors and publicist, this book was a team effort, and I sincerely thank you for your assistance in its birth. To Max Williams, who did my photoshoot for the "About the Author" section. Thank you for your patience and making me look better than I really do. Thanks also for bringing a changing booth and bottle of water for me in the park during our photo shoot in the humid Virginia summer evening time. May the peace of almighty God, which passes all understanding, grant each and every one of you peace, favor, and wisdom as you travel your own path, set forth for you between the bookends of everlasting to everlasting. Amen.

INTRODUCTION

Several years ago, while enjoying a holiday visit from my aunt Dee, who lived in Arizona, she meekly came to my sister and me and asked if, upon her passing, we would be the administrators of her estate. Aunt Dee was a widow, with no children of her own, and certainly not what you'd call a wealthy woman, so she had no one to represent her in this manner. She assured us she had "planned accordingly" and had met with all the appropriate people and had her "affairs in order," and it shouldn't require too much effort due to her advance planning and organization.

Neither my sister nor I had done this type of thing before, but given our fondness for our auntie, we quickly said yes, we would absolutely assist her if that were her wish.

I look back now and think about that day—specifically, how clueless we were with our quick reply and signature on the dotted line. How little thought we gave the question, how quickly we agreed without any research into how these things work or the time it would take to do it, which for us ended up being two years. I do recall thinking, *How bad can it be? She has no children, her home is paid off, everything goes to charity …We'll will write a few checks and make sure her final tax return is done and call it a day.* Today, I smile at how naive we were. How little we knew about the process of tying up loose ends upon someone's death. While we had divine intervention for sure, it was a learning experience. Honestly, I don't know that I would do it again for someone else. Even the cleanest plan took two years to work through. I can't imagine how long it would have taken had Auntie not put her notebook together for us.

You see, Auntie knew she was close to death and came to visit us for Thanksgiving one last time. I'm convinced she knew she would not return home because she brought with her a black, three-ring binder, with tabs that had all the pertinent info in it we would need once she was gone. Before arriving in Richmond, she had cancelled her return transportation and conveniently returned all her oxygen tanks to the local Arizona provider and did not bring any with her for the flight, getting around the airport, or to be with her at my parents' home. In her black binder, there was a cover page of "who to call," their relationship to her (i.e., friend, neighbor, pastor, cousin). It had her medical history and who should take the dog. There were sections that contained her will, and business cards for her insurance man, banker, lawyer. It was indeed a helpful start. This book is a compilation of her original work but also contains information we found, after her passing, was left out. But who could know, if you've never done it? There are things you just didn't know. We dealt with each barrier as it came up, so I've added them to this book and believe it probably covers 98 percent of what you will experience. Just remember, patience, organization, and faithfulness to the preparer's wishes should always come first. Good accounting and records will make it clean and auditable if you indeed get audited by IRS, family, charities, or others who may protest your decisions. Let the book be your guide. If you find anything that's not in my book, feel free to drop me an e-mail with your permission to share and I'll try to add it to the next revision. Thanks, everyone! I hope this workbook is helpful.

1

The Preparer Role versus the Administrator Role

The overall idea is this: Someone will prepare his or her book, the preparer. This is the person who will pass away one day (usually *you*). Once prepared, the book will be given to someone who will have to take care of things upon the preparer's death. That second person, I'm calling the administrator.

The preparer will complete the workbook and insert the recommended document, notes, business cards, etc., and make the administrator aware of where to find the book upon his or her passing.

While the preparer is alive, the book can be a living document that is updated from time to time, however informally that may be. For instance, if I put a copy of my quarterly 401k statement into my workbook, I may not continue to put each new monthly statement into the book as it arrives in the mail each month, but I at lease have it in the book to give my administrator a clue that I have it, what the account number is, and which financial institution has it. The actual balance may be more or less upon my death. That's not important. What is important is that my administrator knows I have it and where to look to get the proceeds from it. The same would go for any credit card statements. The preparer may owe more or less than the current monthly statement he or she originally put into the workbook. Again that's not important, but the statement is there to alert the administrator to the fact that there is a credit card balance, of some amount, that will need to be taken care of, and of course the account closed down after the balance is paid in full. The specific balances and service charges or termination fees will be found when you go to pay off the bill and close the account.

The administrator will use the preparer's workbook as the platform on which to keep all documentation generated while in the throes of administering the estate. They can make notes of dates, times, people to whom they speak about any subject, and what was the conversation or action items. The worksheets pages in the back of the book may be used for calendar entries, reminders, and keeping track of the time you spent on particular tasks. If this person will be looking for reimbursement for their services, the expense reports are a good idea to document properly for audit purposes. If there is more than one administrator (i.e., two or more coadministrators), they may want to set some ground rules about approving each other's expenses prior to beginning this journey. That will keep everyone on the same page. My sister and I agreed on day one that we would approve each other's expense reports and that we would never write checks to ourselves. I would approve her expense report and write her a reimbursement check, and likewise, she would approve my expense reports and write me any reimbursement checks. We also agreed that if we did not have a legible receipt, no reimbursement would be made.

To the preparer, I say, start now. Turn to the back of the book, tear out the shopping list, and head to the office supply store. Once you're home, waste no time assembling your notebook, and for the next month, open your mail, pay your bills, and then three-hole punch them and put them into your workbook under the proper tab. Same for your bank statements and other investment statements; open them, and then instead of filing them or shredding them, three-hole punch them and insert them into your workbook. You have no idea how helpful this is going to be to your administrator one day. Trust me, even though you are gone, your administrator will thank you for your diligence in helping him or her help you.

To the administrator I say, the unfortunate event, however merciful it may be, that will set all this workbook into motion for you is the passing of someone you love. With that, accept my sincerest sympathy for your loss ahead of time. Death is a difficult process to work through. But in dedication to the lost loved one, dedicate yourself to work through this process in good faith and with your best efforts to implement his or her final wishes in a respectful manner. This can be your last good deed to your loved one and he or she will appreciate your effort and time and know that you did your best. I'm sure you will appreciate the help your loved one thought to provide you as you undertake this last task for him or her. Working through this process for someone else will also show you how important it is for you to start your own book for your future. Lastly, may your loved one rest in peace, and may the peace of God that passes all understanding be with you over the next year or so as you do the work ahead.

PREPARER'S SECTION

My Personal Information

Turn to the appendix section in the back of the book. Locate and complete the fields on the worksheet labeled "My Personal Information." This info should include your legal name, not your nickname or shortened version of your name. Your administrator will use this info when completing legal notices after your death so legal accuracy is important.

My Legal Documents

You will want to *make photocopies* of original documents for this workbook. *Do not put your original copies in the book.* All original documents should be kept in either a safety deposit box at your bank or in a safe, fireproof box in your home somewhere. Having copies of documents in the workbook will give your administrator easy access to review when questions arise but will protect the originals for legal use. If you have business cards for any of these people, it's good to add it because it will have many ways to contact them on the card (i.e., phone, fax, e-mail, mobile, physical and mailing addresses).

Photocopies of documents you will want to add:

- will
- medical power of attorney
- trustee/administrator info
- living will
- advanced medical directives
- life insurance policies
- do not resuscitate (DNR) document
- HIPPA privacy forms
- stock certificates
- your own birth certificate
- death certificates (your parents, your spouse, your children—not your own. Your administrator will get that and insert it into their part of the workbook after your death.)
- any prearranged funeral documents you may have
- cemetery plot deed if you own one already

My Contact List

You may use the contact list worksheet in the appendix section of the book to assist with creating your list. This is not the list of emergency contacts (the immediate family/friend list of who to call upon your death) but those people your administrator will need to know in order to close out your affairs.

This list should include people like:

- your life insurance agent
- health insurance agent
- CPA or accountant
- real estate agent you trust to list your home if it will need to be sold
- business partners if you own your own business
- pastor, priest, or other clergy
- banker and banking institution
- stock broker
- funeral home you prefer be used upon your death
- cemetery where you would like to be interned

My Password List

I cannot stress the importance of this section enough. While you have tried your hardest to keep these passwords secret your entire life, it is now time that your administrator knows what they are. I can promise you, the administrator's job will be hard enough without having to fight tech support people for passwords that admittedly are not theirs. Passwords you don't even think about become barriers for your administrators, adding days and even weeks to their process time. Trust me, protect this list while you are alive, but give them a break and show them everything upon your death. Passwords they will need include:

- if you live in a gated community, your code to the gate
- if you have gates in front of your home, the estate gate code
- garage door
- home security system
- home answering machine
- cell phone security code
- cell phone voice mail password
- desktop PC security code
- security codes to specific software or applications on your devices
- laptop security code
- tablet security code
- home Wi-Fi network codes
- debit card PIN
- ATM card PIN
- online banking login and passwords
- online investment login and passwords (i.e., E*TRADE or others)
- Facebook login and password
- Twitter login and password
- LinkedIn login and password
- If you have common residential mailboxes, which box is yours and where is the key.

- car keys

- house keys

- office keys

- safety deposit box location and keys

- In-home safe code or keys

- PIN numbers you used to set up any of your utilities

- login and password info to any online dating sites, like Match.com, eHarmony

- login and password to any online shopping sites, like Amazon

- login and password to online media streaming accounts, like Netflix

ASSET SECTION

Okay, you're making progress. There is more to gathering this info than you thought, isn't it? Can you imagine your poor administrator just having to guess at all this? Pretty overwhelming task it would be, wouldn't it? Well let's help them find all your assets in this section.

This is a pretty simple section to complete. I recommend that starting today and continuing for the next couple of months, you open every bank statement that comes in the mail or electronically, and after reviewing it as normal, you three-hole punch it and add it to this asset section of your workbook. Your goal is to have at least one monthly statement for each asset you have. Mind you, some of your statements only come quarterly, so don't forget about those. Putting the statement itself into the workbook will show your administrator the banking institution, the account number, the phone number of the institution, and a balance of some kind. Remember, the exact balance may or may not be the same at the time of your death. Not important. Knowing there is some money somewhere that will need to be collected and used to pay your bills is the idea with this task. So, go ahead and get started. Some ideas of statements to include are:

- checking account statement
- savings account statement
- 401k/IRA statement
- real estate deeds (remember, copies only; originals to be kept in safety deposit box)
- vehicle titles (photocopies only, originals to safety deposit box)
- stock certificates

LIABILITY SECTION

The idea of the liability section is similar to that of the asset section. You will put at least one monthly statement representing each debt you have into this section of your workbook to give your administrator a clue that you owe some balance to a particular debtor. You don't have to update it every month. Just put it in the book so your administrator will know there is an account at a certain location, with an amount greater than, less than, or equal to the statement in the book.

Samples of liability statements would be:

- car loan
- credit cards
- mortgage statement
- line of credit statement
- student loan statement
- retail store credit cards (i.e., Target, Kohl's, Sears, JCPenny, Old Navy)

This would also be a great place to list any recurring charges that show up on your credit card monthly, like: Netflix, online dating services, cosmetics that automatically show up at your home monthly, monthly book club, tanning salon membership, etc.

Do you own rental property with an active tenant lease? If so, the lease will survive you. That is to say, your administrator cannot kick your tenants out when you pass away in order to sell the home. In most states, the lease survives you, and the tenant is allowed to remain in place until the original lease expires, and sufficient notice must be given alerting to the fact that the lease will not be renewed. So, please, put any copies of active leases into the book so your administrator will know for how long they will need to keep and manage the property in good order after you pass

UTILITIES SECTION

This section is more important than you might think upon first inspection. The reason is that *these bills will continue to accrue even after your death, until someone stops their service.* They will not be cut off immediately after your death. The power and water and maybe telephone will stay in service for some period of time such that the administrator may properly shut down your home.

Your administrator will need to be mindful of just cutting things off too soon, because they will need electrical power and heating/air conditioning in the home if a furniture auction or garage sale will be needed or if there will be people inside the home cleaning out clothes, food, etc. Heat should be kept on as well so pipes don't freeze during the winter months.

Likewise, the water will need to remain for some duration after death, in order that the home may be sufficiently cleaned and the people doing that work may have access to water and bathroom facilities.

In this section, you will place copies of all of your utility bills, such as:

Electric bill

- water bill
- telephone bill
- mobile phone bill
- Internet bill
- cable TV bill
- oil bill
- natural gas bill
- garbage pickup
- lawn care invoice
- pool service company

How to update this workbook

In order for your notebook to be most helpful, you will need to update it from time to time.

It may be that you have paid off a credit card, or gotten a new one, or you may change your cell phone carrier or Internet TV. Whatever is the change, simply put the newest statement in the book and cross out the old statement with a handwritten note that you switched service from one to another and approximately the date you did that.

Same goes for your stock accounts. You may have listed several stocks you owned originally, but over time you sold one or purchased others. A quick handwritten note and copy of new statement will suffice.

Updates don't have to be super formal. Just bear in mind that you are giving someone who has no knowledge about your private affairs a heads-up or clue so they can pursue it and bring it to closure. If you'll just stop and ask yourself, "Would that be helpful information for my administrator?" is usually good enough. More info is better than less info, any day.

ADMINISTRATOR'S SECTION

The general order of things:

A death occurs—go ahead now and look for the preparer's section of the *'Til Death Do We Part* notebook.

The body is recovered by police, medical examiner, or funeral director.

If deemed necessary the medical examiner will perform an autopsy and then release the body to funeral home or organ donation.

There will be a funeral service or memorial service and then a burial or cremation.

The death certificate will be issued, usually after about ten days, and the local courthouse will have it

Change the mailing address to your home immediately. Note the date of change. It only lasts ninety days, and you may need to renew it. This can be done easily enough at the post office.

Go to the home and remove any papers that look like important tax info.

Try to access all messages, voicemail, and e-mail.

Notify Social Security immediately. If preparer was getting monthly SS checks, the SS Admin will want back any checks they sent after the deceased passed, so don't deposit them and think you can keep them. You can't.

Cancel life insurance and health insurance and claim the beneficiary benefits. If the designated beneficiary isn't you or the estate itself, but an actual person or persons, the insuring company will issue beneficiary checks directly to the designated beneficiary without any assistance from you, other than a death certificate copy perhaps.

You may want to have an estate sale to get rid of all furniture and contents of home.

Put the house on the market after the estate sale, if the preparer was not leaving the house to any specific person.

Cancel credit cards—you can't use them for purchases after your loved one's death. That's illegal.

Cancel *unnecessary* utilities like cable TV and cell phone, being careful to leave *on* the water and power. These will be needed until the house is sold

Get in touch with the banker and get your name onto checking and savings accounts.

Get in touch with the CPA and let them know that you will be working with them on the final tax return. Don't be surprised if you end up doing one or even two annual tax returns after your loved one's passing. That's just how long it takes some times to get all this stuff wrapped up.

Be sure to use the telephone encounter worksheets in the back of the workbook to record every telephone call you have. You will need names and phone numbers to follow up but also to show your due diligence effort at completing each task successfully.

Pay off all credit cards, and pay off any bills that arrive. Hopefully you are not in the red. If so, you will need to keep detailed records and reimburse yourself only after the home has sold.

Work closely with your CPA to determine how much money will go to the charities, being careful to figure in their final prep fees for tax returns and tax advice.

Pay the charities, and then complete the final tax return and be done. Note, we paid the CPA in advance for the final tax return so we would have an exact figure to split between the beneficiaries.

Now let's look at each item in a bit more detail, shall we?

A Death Occurs

If you are reading this book, it is likely because someone you loved has died and asked you to settle his or her earthly affairs after his or her death. Your task will not be an easy one, but accept my condolences and my help by using this book as a guide to getting through the next several months of administration work.

Note this book is not to be considered legal or accounting advice. I am not an attorney or CPA. I am simply someone who has done this before and found little helpful information in the mainstream media to assist me when I did it. I thought I could possibly fill a gap in the lack of information on estate administration. To consult with professionals is the wise thing to do, but I'm convinced that my general layout and worksheets will prove vastly helpful to you as you encounter the people and tasks necessary to settle your deceased loved one's affairs.

Let's start with a review of what he or she has accomplished for you. You should notice that the first part of this book, the "Preparer's Section" has been completed for you. If your loved one was diligent, there should be quite a lot of information to assist you along your journey.

I have added worksheets in the appendix section, located in the back of the book. You can also download any of my worksheets from my webpage if you like.

However, first things first. You have a funeral service of some sort to get through before any administration will take place, so you have breathing room prior to commencing any work. Make sure you are the administrator so you don't step on any toes. You most likely signed a legal document accepting responsibility for this. Otherwise, you may be a child of the deceased and this just somewhat fell on you to complete. Again, check with the laws in your particular state and county prior to starting any admin work of any kind. Once you do start, you will need to keep very detailed records of just about everything you do. My recommendation is to get through the funeral services first, and don't attempt to start administration until you have a completed death certificate from the county courthouse. There isn't much you can do anyway without one, so you have some breathing room.

With that said, when someone dies, he or she is usually either at home or in the hospital. If he or she is in the hospital, the nursing staff or doctor will pronounce him or her dead and take them downstairs to the morgue for pickup by the funeral home.

If he or she is at home, you will need to call 911 if he or she is not in hospice and have the police come to the home. They will call the medical examiner's office to come remove the body from the home. Do not touch the body or disturb the scene. They will want to see the scene as it was at the time of death. Don't be offended when they ask you questions and even ask for the medication box containing all the pills your loved one was taking. This is not personal; it is just standard protocol when a death occurs. When a person dies at home and is not in hospice, it is customary for the body to be taken to the medical examiner's office for inspection. If your loved one's body is taken to the medical examiner's office, it may be necessary for you to go there and identify the body and pick up any personal effects that may have been on the person at the time of death (i.e., wedding ring, earrings, clothing, or things that may have been in his or her pockets). You may also get the pillbox back at this time, but expect it to be empty.

If your loved one is officially in hospice care at the time of death, the nurse will call the police or funeral home. When a loved one is in hospice, death is not usually considered a 911 emergency situation. In most cases, the body may remain in the home for a few hours with time for the family to say good-bye. But usually, the funeral home will come by and pick up the body for burial service preparation.

You may need to provide proper identification of the deceased (i.e., a driver's license or DMV identification card if the person has no driver's license). Check your loved one's wallet for organ donor cards. Keep the wallet. Keep track of the cash in the wallet. This can start your petty cash fund. Use the credit cards as a guide to what bills you should expect, what cards you need to shut down, and also watch to make sure no expenses show up after the time of death. Photos of family and friends may be a good place to start as well when it comes to notifying next of kin and friends if this section of the workbook was not completed by the preparer. It is worth noting that sometimes when a person carries around a photo in his or her wallet, it may not be appropriate to call that person. Check your workbook for the prepared emergency contact list. Carefully look through the wallet for clues to the life that person had. Put the wallet in a safe place. You can decide what to do with it later, along with other personal effects.

If the deceased is an organ donor, you will want to notify the medical examiner or funeral home as soon as possible. You many need to contact the organization to whom organs are being left so they can act in a timely manner to harvest the organs so they can be repurposed in good condition. The donor organization will usually reach out to the proper party to make transport and necessary arrangements. After harvest, the body will be cremated there or returned to the proper place for burial processes to proceed. You will need to produce the organ donor card. If you are the administrator, you should be able to find this within the first few pages of the preparer's workbook. We used my auntie's laminated card to show family that these were her wishes and reminded them that she had the laminated card on her person at time of death, such to say, I've laminated the card so no one can change my wishes. A few family members had their own ideas of how she should be buried since she had never had this discussion with them. Again, we used the card to settle everyone down with proof of her wishes. It didn't make it any easier, but we slept well knowing we were doing what she wanted even if others were not happy about it, and that was our job. Immediately, we realized this was going to be harder and more emotional than we thought. We realized that other people may not understand or agree with everything we were going to have to do and how important documentation would be.

You will need to make proper legal notice that your loved one has passed. This is both for courtesy's sake to friends and family but also to potential creditors that require official notice. Your funeral home will most likely have a template you may use for an obituary. In most cases, they will submit the notice to the newspaper for you, but you must check behind to ensure they do. It is a good idea to keep a copy of the obituary and note the exact days it ran in a local newspaper and also the circulation of that paper. Three days is the normal run time. The fee for this is usually included in the funeral home service fee. You may want to start preparing a letter to send to creditors. Wait until you have an official death certificate to send with your letter, as some of the creditors will not be local.

THE BODY

As mentioned earlier, if your loved one passed in the hospital or at home, the body will be taken to either the medical examiner or the funeral home. If your loved one passes on a weekend, you most likely will not be able to meet with the funeral home director or cemetery until the next business day. Refer to the will first and the preparer's workbook second. In every case, the will should be the control document. The workbook is merely where nonformal details can be recorded. How many days of visitation, the style of visitation or wake, open or closed casket, military honors or other honors should be considered. The type of burial (i.e., internment, cremation, or anatomical donation should be searched out in your documentation so the preparer's wishes may be followed exactly). You will also need to pick out burial clothing to include undergarments and hair pieces. A recent photo will help the beautician team present your loved one as closely to how they looked when last alive. If you are lucky, your preparer has written a letter regarding the type of funeral and whom they wish to perform it, right down to the music. If not, you will want to pick something dignified that represents the deceased's style of clothing and music. The funeral home usually has a piano player on call for such events if you do not know a pianist. The pianist can charge up to $250 to $300 in some cases to play music for the service, which may or may not be included in the funeral home service fees.

Next, notice there is a "Legal Documents" section of the preparer's workbook section. These should be photocopies, not original documents. You can find the originals later. They should be locked up in a safety deposit box or home safe. In some cases the original or certified copies of the original may be needed as you work through the various tasks before you. Make sure you do not accidentally give someone the original. The legal documents that should be represented in the "Legal Documents" section are:

- the last will and testament
- any amendments to the will—super important since the original work may have been amended after a life-changing event like divorce, birth of a child, death of a child …
- trust documentation if a trust was established
- estate administrator documents
- power of attorney documents

Remember: These documents rule every situation and should be read in their entirety prior to starting to administer your loved one's wishes. They are the decision maker for every situation. This workbook is not. If you have any question or any doubt, refer to the will with its amendments. If any areas still remain gray or not mentioned at all, I suggest you consult your legal counsel then bow your head and pray, asking God to reveal to you what decision or action would most closely represent your loved one's most likely wish, then with a clear conscience, move forward.

The Funeral

The funeral and services will be an emotional time, so I don't recommend doing any admin work until you respectfully acknowledge one's life and death with the proper memorial.

The funeral home will assist you with most every detail. They will take the ball and run with it. You will either need to pay for the service out of pocket or create a payment plan. The funeral director and staff will have a meeting with you to go over every detail, from obituary notice to funeral type, music, flowers, visitation, casket, casket bedding, visitation sign-in book, cemetery plot, and internment method.

You will need to pick out burial clothing, to include undergarments and any hair pieces. Typically you won't bury someone with any jewelry. The funeral home may want the deceased's dentures in order to make them look well for viewing. Each funeral home is different.

Again, don't jump the gun and get so anxious to start settling affairs that you do not properly stop and grieve. This will be an important step to your own recovery of losing a loved one. You will have much afterward to do, so be respectful and get through the services.

You will need a death certificate for most anything you will need to do. It will take approximately ten days for the funeral home to process the death certificate and send it to the county records office to be recorded in the public records.

Entering the Deceased's Home

As easy as this sounds, you may encounter some barriers like we did. Our aunt lived in a gated community, several states away. We did not have the gate code, and no one wanted to give it to us, of course, assuming if we were supposed to be in there we would have the code already. You should refer to the passwords section of the preparer's workbook. Hopefully they entered the code for you! If not, you may need to contact the Home Owner's Association and explain the situation. They can usually get you in pretty quickly. Another example would by my father's home. Dad does not live in a gated community, but he does have a gated entry to his personal residence. It has a touchpad on the wing wall. You can manually enter the code on the push-button touch pad. Again, these codes should be in the password section of the preparer's workbook.

Once you gained entry into the community or driveway, hopefully you have a spare key to the home, or know where one can be found. If you don't, you may have kept the key ring your loved one had on their person or in their purse at the time of death. The house key should be on the key ring.

Upon entry, I would recommend a quick walk through, taking photos of everything *prior* to touching anything. Of course if there is a pet of some kind that needs attention, give it the required care and attention, but then get your photos before *you* disturb anything.

After getting my initial photos, try to locate the mailbox. It if isn't at the end of the driveway, it may be down the corner in a public mailbox location. This was the case at my aunt's community. The mailboxes were apartment style. And guess what—the box number didn't match the house number for security purposes. Look for the mailbox key, and see if the number is on the key. If not, try to find a piece of mail in the house that has the box number versus the house number on it. If not, do what we did and ask a neighbor if they knew which mailbox was my aunt's. She did, thank goodness. The mailbox was crammed full of mail. We took it all inside and promptly completed a forwarding address form at the post office to redirect all the mail to my house. That kept me from having to check the box every day, which was a good thing since I live in Virginia and my aunt lived in Arizona. I didn't want to have to make any more trips than necessary across the country to settle affairs. Remember, the forwarding only lasts about ninety days. So grab a renewal form from the post office while you're there. Go ahead and renew it for another ninety days before it runs out so you don't have any gaps.

After getting the mail, we checked the messages on the answering machine. We were lucky and there was an old-school answering machine attached to a land line. Some people don't have answering machines anymore, but they can dial a code on their home phone to access the voicemail box provided by the phone company. Check the password section of the preparer's workbook to locate the voicemail password. If there are messages, picking up the telephone handset usually gives you four quick tones, to alert you to the fact you have voicemail messages. Carefully record each message on the mailbox. This may not mean much to you initially, but every detail can help you down the road.

Checking the home safe was something my aunt wanted us to do right away. We did and removed the contents of the safe promptly. We didn't stop to sort through it while in her home. We put it all in a box and took it back to our hotel room to go through each piece of information she felt strongly enough to put in a fireproof box. Some of it was important, some of it was only important to her, and some of it was just memories she apparently treasured enough to lock away for safekeeping.

You may have complications like we did. There was someone else who apparently had a key to my aunt's home who entered it before we did, and then again after we did. It became necessary for us to post "No Trespassing" signs in the windows, to put everyone on notice that the home was not to be entered again. Our situation was a bit unique and required surveillance until the home was empty and sold.

The next thing we did was search the home for anything that looked like asset statements, bills to be paid, and important tax info. We were lucky in that 95 percent of the info we found was just a duplicate copy of something already in the preparer's section of the workbook. But we did get some statements in the mail not represented in the book. We simply three-hole punched them and added them.

VERIFYING ALL ASSETS

My aunt left us names, phone numbers, and business cards of her asset managers. We quickly called them on the next business day and introduced ourselves. Lucky for us, she had reached out to most of them already, letting them know to expect a call from us and asking them to help us as best they could. This was comforting and helpful on many levels.

We began the process of reconciling the assets in the workbook to the assets we found when meeting with these bankers, brokers, and CPAs. Documentation and signatures were required by most of these professionals to be able to assist us and release these assets to us. In my aunt's case, her estate was the beneficiary for all her assets. Once everything was entered into the estate accounts, bills were paid, and then the remaining balances were distributed to the charities noted in her will. If she had named a specific person as a beneficiary, the funds would have been released to him or her directly, versus the estate.

My aunt had already sold her car as she was unable to drive, so we didn't have to make any arrangements to sell it. You may have a vehicle you need to sell. Don't forget, personal property taxes (if you live in a state like Virginia that has personal property taxes) will still accrue until you sell it. Take the plates off and turn them back into the local DMV, being sure to cancel any driver's licenses. You will need a death certificate to do this. You may get a small refund if the taxes or tags were paid in advance. Just deposit this into the main checking account from which you are working, being sure to keep a copy of the refund check and document it in the checkbook register.

It took thirty to sixty days to get some of the assets cashed out and checks in the mail. This seemed like forever, but perhaps in hindsight that's just a normal business cycle.

My sister and I went through the home, boxing up obvious trash items and getting them to the dump. Actually, we didn't take them to the dump. We bagged them and put them in the garage. We cleaned out the bathrooms and the kitchen. We cleaned the refrigerator, throwing away all perishable foods, most of which was already bad by the time we got to the home.

Because we were out of town, we hired a local fiduciary to perform the estate sale. She was excellent. She priced and tagged all the items in the home for sale, making a detailed list of everything being offered for sale and the price for which it was offered. This list became important when it came time to settle up. For jewelry and collectibles, if she wasn't sure of the price, she had local contacts who appraised items whose value was uncertain to us.

You'd be surprised what people will purchase. Neighbors purchased canned goods right out of the cupboards and unopened toiletries out of the bathrooms. I had no idea people would be looking for these items as well as furniture and things in the garage.

But who knew, the fiduciary produced a list of sold items and a check for their proceeds. She called the waste management service to pick up all the garbage and the charities to pick up any remaining furniture, clothing, and bedding.

After the estate sale, we picked a local Realtor who had experience selling retirement community property. An inspection was done, and small items of repair were noted. We figured we could contract out these repairs or we could leave them and just reduce the selling price. Ultimately we felt it in the best interest to perform the repairs, making the home move-in ready and get as much as we could for the charities

Our fiduciary assisted us with getting the repair estimates. She also assisted in letting the repair vendors into the home to make the repairs. Once all repairs were made and the home was completely empty, we contacted the Realtor and onto the market she went.

We could have just taken the first offer we received, but we negotiated in good faith as we would have if the money had been ours. It actually gave us a huge sense of pride. Instead of making the process faster, we hunkered down and got the charities as much as we could. To this day, I look back and feel good about that.

After the home sold, we had all the assets cashed out and funds were in the checking account. We knew what was next ... paying off the bills. I cannot underestimate the value of working with a CPA. The CPA should be able to help you with the final tax return and the treatment of all charitable contributions as it pertains to that final tax return. After cashing out all assets, paying off all expenses, distribution to charities or dependents, the CPA will prepare the final tax return, also preparing 1099-Misc statements to those who received any cash from the estate. After you prepare that final tax return, the deceased's bank account should be $0.00, and you should be able to close the account and know that your work is finally complete.

Verifying Liabilities and Paying off the Bills

Gather in all your assets before you pay any bills. This is just a good rule of thumb, but timing is of the essence because finance charges will accrue. Late fees will accrue if you delay, and these are hard to negotiate off. So be as prompt as you can in making your assessment. However, once your money is gone, it is gone. So gathering it all in first and understanding your financial position is important.

After a couple of months of making sure we had all recurring statements, we felt we were ready to start paying off some bills.

Carefully review each credit card statement. We found some charges posted several days after my aunt's death. Online purchases were made and charged to her account. How anyone got her information we don't have a clue, but we promptly notified the credit card company and provided a death certificate showing it was impossible that the charges were legit. They were written off and investigated as fraud. Fortunately, the company from which the purchases had been made had the shipping address to where the material went.

Close inspection will also reveal if there are any automatic billings that need to be cancelled—things like Netflix, tanning salon memberships, online dating services, and book Club memberships. Anything that was previously set up to automatically charge the account without a live signature was immediately cancelled. Again, death certificates were required.

UTILITIES

This section is super important, so it has been intentionally pulled out of liabilities section. Some of the utilities can be cancelled immediately. Things that are not necessary, like cable TV and mobile phones, can be cancelled immediately. However, things like electrical power, water, heating, and air may need to stay on even after death until the house is sold. Workers can't come in and clean up if there are no lights, water, or bathroom facilities.

If you live in a cold climate, pipes can freeze if temps drop and you have turned off the heat prematurely. Likewise, it can get too hot and stuffy for an estate sale if the temperature or humidity is high, especially if you live in the South. You may want to continue the lawn care service unless you plan to cut the lawn yourself while going through this process.

When taking back the cable box, remember to take the box, the cables, and the remotes. You will most likely get a credit back that can be applied to the final invoice, lessening your expenses. If they allow you to ship them back, make sure you keep a tracking receipt in the event the boxes need to be traced.

Don't be surprised if you call the utility companies to make them aware of your loved one's passing and they insist you put the utilities in *your* name or they will be turned off. They don't want the bill to continue to run if there is no guarantee they will not get paid. Plus they may get a small fee or deposit to transfer the account into your name. If you choose not to announce to the utility company, they may still see it from the death notice you ran in the paper or they may not. If you don't call them to tell them, you will want to make sure you pay every bill on time so services don't get turned off for nonpayment.

You can usually get the gas company and even the oil company to come and take the unused portion of the product and tank away. This may result in a credit being applied to the final invoice. Again, examine the timing of removing these services.

After the home has sold and you have a closing date, make sure all the utilities turn off that day. This should happen anyway as service should be reconnected in the new owner's name.

Petty Cash Fund

As I'm sure you have noticed by now, there are expenses involved with making all these things happen. A good petty cash fund will assist with a lot of the expenses. Make sure you document any cash added to the fund and any money removed from the fund. There should be matching receipts for every expenditure. Make notes on the back of the receipts if you need to do so.

I recommend starting the petty cash fund with the money you find in the deceased's wallet. Some people also have a jar in which they toss all their coins. This can add up quickly even though it's just change. Roll it and add it to the fund it you need it. The money will be consumed quickly, so you may want to add $100 or so to it as needed. Again, documentation is the key.

Some of the expenses you will incur, like small home repairs prior to putting house on the market, you may be able to negotiate the terms to "payment upon closing on the sale of home." Some vendors will work with you if you tell them the situation.

I have included petty cash journal and petty cash vouchers in appendix B.

Well, friend, you've reached the end of the workbook. While you may be finished reading, I'm assuming much work is still ahead for you. Thank you for taking the time to purchase my book!

I truly hope it is helpful to you!

If you have any questions, please feel free to contact me via my webpage: www. KimberlyJenkinsauthor.com, and I will make every attempt to answer your question to the best of my ability.

If you do use my book, drop me a line and let me know how it went for you. I can't wait to see if my work has been helpful to anyone!

Take care and bye for now!

EPILOGUE

If you were not lucky enough that your loved one completed the preparer section of this book prior to their death, have no fear. It will take more time, but you can complete the section for him or her.

Start collecting all the asset statements and credit card bills and utility bills, and insert them into the workbook yourself. This will actually help you get organized enough to work more efficiently. You'll thank yourself later for the organization and audit trail you created yourself.

Hopefully, too, this will show you how important it is to be prepared. You may even want to start your own book so you can give it to your administrator when it's your turn. Think of all the time and stress you will save him or her.

Good luck to you, and may God bless you in many ways!

APPENDIX A

Preparer's Shopping List

Tear out this sheet (or download from my web page www.kimberlyjenkinsauthor.com) and take it with you to your local office supply store. You will be able to get all your supplies in one trip, which should save you time and money. Don't forget to search online for any coupons that may be available from your local office supply store. Print any you find, and take them with you.

Shopping List

1. Three-ring binder with an envelope on the inside and back flaps. The one that lets you slide a title page on the front is perfect.
2. Twelve divider tabs
3. Two file folder pocket sleeves that you can put into your binder
4. One box of #10 envelopes
5. One book of stamps—get Forever stamps if you can so the value doesn't change on you.
6. One banker's box for storage
7. One box of three-tab file folders
8. One yellow highlighter

When you get back home, label your tabs: Contacts, Assets, Liabilities, Utilities, Will, Death Certificates, Power of Attorney, Photos, Worksheets, Notes. Put all of them into your three-ring binder.

Put the sleeves with pockets into your binder.

Now you're set to get started.

APPENDIX B

Preparer's Forms

SUN	MON	TUE	WED	THU	FRI	SAT

PHONE CALL

	DATE	TIME	BY
NAME			
PHONE NO			

REMARKS:

FOLLOW UP NEEDED:

35

Mileage Log

Total mileage recorded: 34.7

Date	Time	Description	Purpose	From	To	Odometer Start	Odometer Finish	Mileage
						33,489.1	33,521.4	32.3
						33,521.4	33,523.8	2.4
								0.0
								0.0
								0.0
								0.0
								0.0
								0.0
								0.0
								0.0
								0.0
								0.0
								0.0
								0.0
								0.0
								0.0
								0.0
								0.0
								0.0
								0.0
								0.0
								0.0
								0.0
								0.0

Weekly Time Sheet

[Your Name]

[Street Address] [Street Address 2] [City, State/Province, Postal Code]

Week Start:	8/10/2016
Employee:	[Type Name Here]
Manager:	[Type Name Here]
Employee phone:	[Phone]
Employee e-mail:	[E-Mail Address]

Rate per hour: $50.00

Day	Date	Time In	Time Out	Time In 2	Time Out 2	Regular Hours	Overtime (1.5 x rate)	Sick Hours	Vacation Hours	Total Pay
Wednesday	8/10/2016	8:00 AM	11:00 AM	12:00 PM	2:00 PM	5		3		$ 400.00
Thursday	8/11/2016	11:00 PM	3:00 AM	4:00 AM	10:00 AM	8	2			550.00
Friday	8/12/2016	8:00 AM	10:00 AM		10:00 AM	2			6	400.00
Saturday	8/13/2016									-
Sunday	8/14/2016									-
Monday	8/15/2016									-
Tuesday	8/16/2016									-
Total						15	2	3	6	$ 1,350.00

Employee Signature _____   Date _____

Manager Signature _____   Date _____

www.kimberlyjenkinsauthor.com/resources/weeklytimesheet

39

Expense report

PURPOSE: _____

STATEMENT NUMBER: _____

PAY PERIOD: _____

From _____

To _____

EMPLOYEE INFORMATION:

Name _____

Position _____

SSN _____

Department _____

Manager _____

Employee ID _____

Date	Account	Description	Hotel	Transport	Fuel	Meals	Phone	Column1	Entertainment	Misc.	Total
											$ -
											-
											-
											-
											-
											-
											-
											-
											-
											-
											-
											-
											-
	$ -		$ -	$ -	$ -	$ -	$ -	$ -	$ -	$ -	
										Subtotal	$ -
										Advances	

NOTES: _____

APPROVED: _____

PETTY CASH VOUCHER

PAY TO THE ORDER OF _____

DATE _____

AMOUNT OF _____
in words

DESCRIPTION _____

AMOUNT $ _____

APPROVED BY: _____

Date	Check No.	Check Issued to	In Payment of	Amount of check	✔	Date of deposit	Amount of deposit	Balance

APPENDIX C

Administrator's Forms

To-do lists   **Completed by:** [Name]
Deadline: [Date]

Done?	Project 1	Due By	Notes
Yes	Planning	●	9/5/10
Yes	Preparation	●	4/18/10
No	Task a	●	4/18/11
	Task b		
	Task c		
	Task d		
	Paperwork		
	Hand-off		
	Follow-up		

Done?	Project 2	Due By	Notes
Yes	Planning	●	9/5/10
Yes	Preparation	●	4/18/10
No	Task a	●	4/18/11

Done?	Project 3	Due By	Notes
Yes	Planning	●	9/5/10
Yes	Preparation	●	4/18/10
No	Task a	●	4/18/11

NOTES

Sample Letter to Creditor

Date

Creditor name

Address

City state, zip

Re: Notice of the death of (name of the deceased)
        Account #

To Whom it may concern,

My name is (your name). I am writing to you to inform you of the death of my loved one, (name of the deceased). I have been named the Executor of his/her estate and am trying to settle the above account# with you.

I have enclosed a copy of the death certificate and request that the account be closed immediately and the final statement be sent to me that I may settle the balance with you as quickly as may be.

If there is any way to put a hold on any finance charges that may accrue while I am in the process of closing the estate it would be greatly appreciated.

Should you need to contact me, I may be reached at: (address and telephone number).

Thank you for your assistance,

(your name and telephone number)

INFORMATION REQUIED FOR DEATH CERTIFICATE

	First	Middle	Last	Maiden
Full Name				
SSN		DOB:		SEX Male( ) Female ( )
Citizen of USA?	Yes ( ) No ( )	City & State of Birth:		
Race	Caucasian( ) African American ( ) Asian( ) Specify:			
	American Indian ( ) Tribe:			
Hispanic Origin: No( ) Yes( ) Specify:_____				
Father's Name:			State of birth:	
Mother's Name			State of birth:	
Highest level of Education:	in years:	Degree: No Degree ( ), HS Diploma ( ), GED ( ), A.A ( ) BS/BA ( ), Masters ( ), PhD. ( )		
Military Service: No ( ) Yes ( ) Branch:				
Occupation/Job title:	Please list only ONE			
Industry:		Years in occupation:		
Donor's Address:	Street and Number			
City:	State:		Zip:	
Inside city Limits? Yes ( ) No ( )		County:	Years in county	
Marital Status:	Never Married ( ), Married ( ) Widowed ( ) Divorced ( )			
Spouse's Name:			If wife give maiden name	
Nexf of kin (NOK):			Relation to donor:	
NOK address:				
City:	State:		Zip:	
Phone:	Cell:			

ESTATE SALE INVENTORY LIST

DATE:

ADDRESS:

CITY:

STATE

ZIP

PIC?	APPRAISAL?	ITEM (INCLUDE MFG MAKE/MODEL/YEAR IF NECESSARY)	LISTED PRICE	ACCEPTED PRICE
		TOTAL		

55

CONTACT LIST:

COMPANY NAME	CONTACT NAME	CONTACT TITLE	CONTACT ADDRESS	CITY	STATE	ZIP	PHONE #	FAX #	EMAIL

WWW.KIMBERLYJENKINSAUTHOR.COM

OFFICE SUPPLY

Shopping List:

1. 3 ring binder with an envelope on the inside and back flaps
   The one that lets you slide a title page under the front cover is perfect
2. 12 divider tabs
3. 2 file folder pocket sleeves that you can put into your binder
4. 1 box of #10 envelopes
5. 1 book of stamps – get "Forever" stamps if you can so the value doesn't change on you
6. 1 Banker's box for storage
7. 1 box of 3 tab file folders
8. 1 yellow hi liter
9. Three hole punch
10. Pens

ABOUT THE AUTHOR

Born in Richmond, Virginia, in 1965 to a policeman and housewife, Kimberly grew up with one older sister. She attended a small private Christian school from the third grade until she completed her high school education a year early by skipping eleventh grade. She was a track and field star in high school, winning blue ribbons in every event, short distance and long distance. She fondly tells the story of believing she was good until she barely made the track team at the University of Richmond. "There were girls who could run hurdles faster that I could run straightaways right beside them. I quickly learned I was only a big fish in a little pond at the Christian academy and that there was a whole world out there of girls who were as good and better than me. It was a humbling life lesson that built character in me."

Married to her high school sweetheart at the age of twenty-four, Kim has one daughter who is now twenty-six and married to her own high school sweetheart of ten years. Of her daughter, she says with a glowing smile on her face, "If my daughter was the only blessing God ever gave me, should would have been more than I ever deserved."

At the age of twenty-seven, Kimberly started her own telecommunications company, installing complex communications systems into hospitals and assisted living facilities, interfacing them to life safety systems, all over North America. Kimberly enjoyed her company for nearly twenty years before executing her exit strategy, selling it, and retiring at the age of forty-eight. She enjoys motivating others to make their dreams come true and cheerleading them along their own road.

After some post-retirement travel throughout Europe, she settled again in Chesterfield County, Virginia. To fill her time while waiting for grandbabies, she entered a technical college and studied the basics of nursing and now works for a family practice in Colonial Heights. "When my first grandchild arrives, being a Nanny will be my next full-time job. I just can't wait."

She also has a real estate investment company with her daughter. They enjoy buying and renovating houses in their spare time. "It's fun, and I love working with my daughter. She's an excellent business partner, and it's great for me because I get to spend more time with her, call it work, and make some money doing it. I hope she never catches on that I just do it spend even more time with her."

Kimberly lives in Chesterfield, Virginia, with her two English bulldogs, Rupert and LuLu, and is currently writing her second book, a Bible study on the Old Testament book of Nehemiah, which should be out in the fall of 2017.

AUNT DEE'S SWEET POTATO CASSEROLE

2 (40-oz) cans of mashed sweet potato
1 (26.9-oz) can mashed sweet potato
¾ cup sugar
2 eggs
1 tsp. vanilla
1/3 cup whole milk
½ cup melted butter

Whip together all ingredients, and put into a casserole dish. Top with brown sugar topping—see below.

Brown Sugar Topping
1 cup brown sugar
1/3 cup flour
1/3 cup butter
1 cup chopped pecans

Combine all ingredients in small mixing brown, and sprinkle on top of casserole. Bake thirty minutes at 350 degrees.

Note: This is the casserole Aunt Dee made us every Thanksgiving and Christmas.

Printed in the United States
By Bookmasters